Nelson Comprehension

Pupil Book

2

Wendy Wren
Series Editor: John Jackman

Nelson Thornes

Published in 2009 by:
Nelson Thornes Ltd
Delta Place
27 Bath Road
CHELTENHAM
GL53 6TH
United Kingdom

11 12 13 / 10 9 8 7 6 5 4 3 2

A catalogue record for this book is available from the British Library

ISBN 978 1 4085 0547 2

Illustrations by: Maurizio De Angelis, Robin Lawrie, Wes Lowe, Ivan Vazquez and Topics

Photographs courtesy of: Alamy pp10, 11, 12, 13, 23, 51, 54, 55; Barcroft Media p14; BBC Photo Library for photo by Douglas Playle used on the front cover of John Christopher, *The Tripods Trilogy* Copyright © BBC p48; Fotolia pp24, 26, 27, 34

Page layout by Topics – The Creative Partnership, Exeter

Printed in China by 1010 Printing International Ltd

Acknowledgements

The author and publishers wish to thank the following for permission to use copyright material:

[Unit 7 Talk] The Agency (London) Ltd on behalf of the author for material from Beverley Naidoo, *Journey to Jo'burg*, Longman Group (1985) pp. 42–3. Copyright © Beverley Naidoo 1985; [Unit 3 Talk] Atheneum Books for Young Readers, an imprint of Simon & Schuster Children's Publishing Division, for Rachel Fields, 'The Hills' from *Poems* by Rachel Field. Copyright © 1934 Macmillan Publishing Company, copyright renewed © 1962 Arthur S Pederson; [Unit 1 Write] Laura Cecil Literary Agency on behalf of the Estate of the author for material from Robert Westall, *Blitz*, Collins (1994) pp. 15–8. Copyright © Robert Westall 1985; [Unit 9 Write & Unit 10 Teach] The C S Lewis Company Ltd for material from C S Lewis, *The Lion, the Witch and the Wardrobe*, Collins (1980) pp. 13–5. Copyright © C S Lewis Pte Ltd 1950; [Unit 1 Teach & Unit 10 Write] Curtis Brown Group Ltd London on behalf of the author for material from Nina Bawden *Carrie's War*, Gollancz (1975) pp. 12–4. Copyright © Nina Bawden 1973; [Unit 5 Talk] Faber and Faber Ltd for material from Kenneth Lillington, *The Hallowe'en Cat* (1987) pp. 1–2; [Unit 3 Write] David Harmer for his poem, 'One Moment In Summer'; [Unit 3 Teach & Unit 9 Teach] David Higham Associates on behalf of the authors for material from Jill Paton Walsh, *Shine*, Macdonald and Co (1988) pp. 26–8; and Berlie Doherty, 'Quieter Than Snow' from *Walking on Air* by Berlie Doherty, Hodder Children's Books (1999); [Unit 5 Teach & Unit 10 Talk] Orion Children's Books, London for material from Alan Gibbons, *Chicken*, Dent Children's Books (1993) pp. 5–7; [Unit 5 Write] Pearson Education for material from George Layton, 'The Balaclava Story' from *The Fib and other Stories* by George Layton, The Longman Group (1975); [Unit 8 Talk] Penguin Books Ltd for logo and typography of front cover and back blurb of John Christopher, *The Tripods Trilogy*, Puffin Books (1984); [Unit 7 Teach] Rogers, Coleridge & White Ltd on behalf of the author for material from Anita Desai, *The Peacock Garden*, Heineman (1979) pp. 5–7. Copyright © 1979 Anita Desai; [Unit 7 Write] Trident Media Group on behalf of the author for material from Ann Cameron, *The Most Beautiful Place in the World*, Transworld (1988) pp.11–6. Copyright © 1988 by Ann Cameron.

Every effort has been made to trace the copyright holders but if any have been inadvertently overlooked the publishers will be pleased to make the necessary arrangement at the first opportunity.

Contents

Leaving London

Carrie, 12, and her younger brother Nick, 9, are being evacuated from London during the Second World War. They are on a train with their schoolteacher, Miss Fazackerly, going to Wales.

He threw up all over Miss Fazackerly's skirt. He had been feeling sick ever since they left the main junction and climbed into the joggling, **jolting** little train for the last lap of their journey, but the sudden whistle had **finished him**.

Such a noise – it seemed to split the sky open. 'Enough to frighten the dead,' Miss Fazackerly said, mopping her skirt and Nick's face with her handkerchief. He lay back limp as a rag and let her do it, the way he always let people do things for him, **not lifting a finger**. 'Poor lamb,' Miss Fazackerly said, but Carrie looked **stern**.

'It's all his own fault. He's been stuffing his face ever since we left London. Greedy pig. *Dustbin.*'

He had not only eaten his own packed lunch – sandwiches and cold sausages and bananas – but most of Carrie's as well. She had let him have it to comfort him because he minded leaving home and their mother more than she did. Or had looked as if he minded more. She thought now that it was just one of his acts, put on to get **sympathy**. Sympathy and chocolate! He had had all her chocolate, too! 'I knew he'd be sick,' she said **smugly**.

'Might have warned me then, mightn't you?' Miss Fazackerly said. Not unkindly, she was one of the kindest teachers in the school, but Carrie wanted to cry suddenly. If she had been Nick she would have cried, or at least put on a hurt face. Being Carrie she stared crossly out of the carriage window at the big mountain on the far side of the valley. It was brown and purple on the top and green lower down; streaked with silver trickles of water and dotted with sheep.

Sheep and mountains. 'Oh, it'll be such fun,' their mother had said when she kissed them good-bye at the station. 'Living in the country instead of the **stuffy** old city. You'll love it, you see if you don't!' As if Hitler had arranged this old war for their benefit, just so that Carrie and Nick could be sent away in a train with gas masks slung over their shoulders and their names on cards round their necks. Labelled like parcels – Caroline Wendy Willow and Nicholas Peter Willow – only with no address to be sent to. None of them, not even the teachers, knew where they were going. 'That's part of the adventure,' Carrie's mother had said, and not just to cheer them up: it was her **nature** to **look on the bright side**. If she found herself in Hell, Carrie thought now, she'd just say, 'Well, at least we'll be *warm.*'

Thinking of her mother, always making the best of things (or pretending to: when the train began to move she had stopped smiling), Carrie nearly did cry. There was a lump like a pill stuck in her throat. She swallowed hard and pulled faces.

The train was slowing. 'Here we are,' Miss Fazackerly said. 'Collect your things, don't leave anything. Take care of Nick, Carrie.'

Carrie's War, Nina Bawden

- Who are the main characters in the story?
- What is the setting?
- We are told that Miss Fazackerly is kind. What kind things does she do?
- Why has Nick been sick?
- Where are they moving to?
- Where are they moving from?
- Explain the meaning of the words and phrases in **bold**.
- What impression do you get of:
  - Carrie
  - Nick
  - their mother?
- Why do you think the children are being sent away from home?
- If you were Nick or Carrie, would you think this was an adventure or would you be homesick? Give your reasons.

5

Dad's double

In September 1939 the Second World War began. Freddy's father leaves to fight in the war and Freddy may never see him again. He watched the enemy planes fly over the town and saw the American soldiers arrive. One day, some other people came …

There were other new arrivals. But they didn't come into the town. Freddy and Stella were walking along the road which passed Farmer Crellin's outlying fields when they saw them. A group of six men, their backs bowed, repairing fences. They wore shabby grey tunics with a yellow circle stitched on the back of each one. A soldier with a rifle stood guarding them. He motioned Stella and Freddy away.

One of the men looked up and stared straight at Freddy.

Freddy's stomach turned over and his legs felt like water.

The man was exactly like his father.

'Da … ' he started to call. But he cut the word off at once.

The man showed no sign of recognition. His face was lined and bitter. Voices murmured. Freddy knew they were speaking in German.

'I'm frightened,' said Stella. 'Let's go home.'

Understanding the passage

● What were the men doing when Freddy and Stella first saw them?

● What was unusual about one of the men?

● What language were they speaking?

● What did Mr Binstead think of prisoners of war?

● What did Freddy dream about?

Looking at words

Explain the meaning of the expressions as they are used in the story:

a stomach turned over   **b** serve 'em right

Mum was weeding in the back garden when he returned. Grandads Crake and Bassett were there as well, arguing. Granny Bassett sat in a deck-chair, trying not to listen. Mr Binstead was digging his garden next door. Freddy told them what he'd seen, without mentioning Dad's German double.

'German prisoners of war,' said Mum. 'A few are allowed to work on farms. You must keep away from them.'

Mr Binstead heard.

'A waste of good food,' he shouted over the fence. 'We can do without that lot. If I had my way, they'd all be shot. Serve 'em right after what they've done to us.'

Mum ran indoors, crying.

'Oh, sorry,' said Mr Binstead. 'I forgot.'

'He's a right twerp,' said Grandad Crake.

'He ought to be shot himself,' said Grandad Bassett.

At least they agreed for once. Freddy dreamed most nights now of his father in a grey tunic working by the side of a road and lines of tanks with white stars on them coming to take him away. And at the back of his dreams was the face of Dad's German double – thin, lined, stubbly-chinned, but with the bitterness in the eyes replaced by yearning at the thought of the many miles between him and his home.

The War and Freddy, Dennis Hamley

Explain the meaning of these words:

a outlying   **b** shabby   **c** recognition

d twerp   **e** bitterness   **f** yearning

Exploring further

● Why do you think the men had a yellow circle stitched on the back of their tunics?

● Why do you think Stella was frightened?

● Why do you think Freddy didn't mention 'Dad's German double'?

● Why do you think Freddy's mum ran indoors crying?

● Do you think Freddy agreed with Mr Binstead? Why? Why not?

Extra

Imagine you could talk to the German who looked like Freddy's dad. What do you want to know about him? What questions would you ask?

The crash

Albert and the narrator are young boys during the Second World War. One day they are playing on an abandoned building site known as Kor. They see a fight in the sky between a German and a British plane. One of the planes crashes …

'Shall we go and look?'

'He might be trapped … He might be …'

It was unsayable. But we went.

It took a long time to search ruined Kor. Expecting at every corner …

But what we found was a surprisingly long way off. A new row of furrows in the field beyond Kor, as if a farmer with six ploughs joined together had …

And a gap in the hedge that something had vanished through. Something definitely British, because a lump of the tail had fallen off, and lay with red, white and blue on it.

We tiptoed through the gap.

It looked as big as a house.

'Spitfire.'

'Hurricane, you idiot. Can't you tell a Spitfire from a Hurricane yet?'

'It's not badly damaged. Just a bit bent.'

I shook my head. 'It'll never fly again. It looks … broke.'

The tail was up in the air; the engine dug right into the ground, and the propeller bent into horseshoe shapes.

'Where's the pilot?'

'He might have baled out,' suggested Albert, hopefully.

'What? At that height? His parachute would never have opened. Reckon he's trapped inside. We'd better have a look.'

'Keep well back,' said Albert. 'There's a terrible smell of petrol. I saw petrol take fire once …'

There was no point in mocking him. I was so scared my own legs wouldn't stop shaking. But it was me that went a yard in front.

The cockpit canopy was closed. Inside, from a distance, there was no sign of any pilot.

'Baled out. Told ya,' said Albert.

'With the canopy closed?'

'The crash could've closed it, stupid.'

'I'm going to have a look.'

I don't think I would have done if I'd thought there was anybody inside. I edged up on the wing, frightened that my steel toe and heel caps would strike a spark from something. The smell of petrol was asphyxiating.

He was inside.

Bent up double, with only the back of his helmet showing. And there was a great tear in the side of the helmet, with leather and stuffing … and blood showing through.

Blitz, Robert Westall

Understanding the passage

1 What were the boys going to look for?

2 How did the boys know that what had 'vanished through' the hedge was 'definitely British'?

3 What are a Hurricane and a Spitfire?

4 What did the narrator see in the cockpit?

Looking at words

5 Explain the meaning of the words and phrases as they are used in the extract:

   a unsayable   **b** vanished   **c** baled out

   d edged up   **e** asphyxiating

Exploring further

6 Why do you think the author left these sentences unfinished:

   a 'He might be …'   **b** 'Expecting at every corner …'

7 Why does the narrator say, 'His parachute would never have opened'?

8 The narrator says, 'I was so scared …' What two things do you think he was scared of?

9 Both the boys were frightened but which of them do you think was braver? Why?

10 How would you have felt if you were one of the boys? What would you have done?

Extra

Imagine you are the narrator. What would you do and how would you feel if:

a you found the pilot dead **b** you found the pilot injured but alive?

No Rest For Marathon Marvel!

Tom Phillips
Sport **Correspondent**

Paula Radcliffe is the world marathon record holder. She ran the 26 miles of the 2002 London Marathon in a record-breaking 2 hours, 18 minutes and 56 seconds. Later in the year, Paula won the Chicago Marathon, breaking her own record by 1 minute, 29 seconds. The British public **took Paula to their hearts** and voted her BBC Sports Personality of the Year.

Born in 1973, in Cheshire, Paula suffered from asthma and **anaemia** as a child.

Despite this she took up running at the age of seven and joined the Frodsham Athletic Club. At the age of 12, her family moved to Bedfordshire and she joined the Bedford Athletic Club. In 1992, she won the world junior title, and in 2001 the World Cross Country Championships.

Paula, now 35, shows no sign of stopping. Her first major race this year will be the London Marathon on 26th April. She had to **withdraw** from this race in 2008 due to a foot injury and she is very keen to win it again.

While Christmas and New Year is a time when most people relax, Paula started her **intensive** training. She spent three weeks in France, running on snow in the mountains. From there she is travelling to New Mexico for eight more weeks of training. She hopes to run either a ten-kilometre or a half-marathon race in America as part of her **preparations** for the London Marathon.

Fans of the sport are keen to see Paula **back in action**. Kim Thomas, who has seen every London Marathon and travels to watch Paula run all over the world said, 'She is truly amazing. It takes such strength and **determination** to compete as she does. I think long-distance running must be the hardest sport there is.'

The *Daily Express* recognises that 'she deserves her place as one of the world greats of athletics' and the *Daily Mail* claims she is 'Britain's greatest ever woman athlete'. Few would say they are wrong.

- What is the article about?
- What is so special about Paula Radcliffe?
- Why did she not compete in the 2008 London Marathon?
- What do the *Daily Express* and the *Daily Mail* think about Paula?
- Explain the meaning of the words and phrases in **bold**.
- In what time did Paula run the Chicago marathon?
- Why do you think Paula trains by running on snow?
- How do you know that Kim Thomas is a keen fan of the sport?
- Do you think it is a good headline? Why? Why not?
- How many paragraphs are there in the article? What is each one about?
- Give an example from the article of a fact and an opinion.

ON YOUR BIKE!

Sally Davis Transport Correspondent

Pedestrians do not like bicycles on the pavement. Drivers do not like bicycles on the road. But love them or hate them, cyclists are not only here to stay but are increasing in number at a rapid rate.

In London, journeys on bicycles have doubled since 2000 and now stand at more than half a million a day. Sheffield has also seen a 50 per cent rise in the use of bicycles since 2001.

So what is causing people to leave their cars at home, shun public transport and get on their bikes? Over the years, the cost of petrol going up and up is one reason, along with the difficulty and cost of parking. Another reason is the time it takes to get to work using public transport.

Understanding the article

- Who wrote the article?
- What is it about?
- How many bicycle journeys are there each day in London?
- How many reasons does the article give for people using bicycles? What are they?

Looking at words

Explain the meaning of these words as they are used in the article:

a pedestrians   **b** rapid   **c** shun

d delayed   **e** cancelled   **f** concern

Exploring further

- Why do you think:

  a pedestrians do not like cyclists   **b** drivers do not like cyclists?

- What can the expression 'on your bike' sometimes mean? What does it mean here?

Buses are often late and trains can be delayed or cancelled. Some people say it is a concern for the planet as they think cycling is 'greener' than transport that uses petrol and diesel.

Recently, however, there is another reason. Whilst cycling has been popular in many countries for a long time, it was the success of the British Cycling Team at the Olympics in 2008 that made people become enthusiastic about cycling. Having won eight gold medals (14 in all) the team have inspired people, and thousands have bought and are using the type of bicycle that Chris Hoy and the team won their medals on.

The Government is also doing its bit.

It plans to spend £100 million to improve cycling in 12 cities. This means more cycle lanes, cycle training at school and a scheme where old bicycles will be repaired and given to people who cannot afford them.

- The article gives reasons for why people are using bicycles. Which do you think is the best reason? Why?
- How many medals that were not gold did the British Cycling Team win?
- Give an example from the article of a fact and an opinion.
- Do you think cycle training is a good idea or not?

Extra

Your school is going to begin cycle training lessons. Design a leaflet for parents telling them:

a when and where the training will be

b why it is important that children learn to ride a bicycle properly

c why cycling is good for the environment.

You want people to read it and not just throw it away. Think of a good headline and make the leaflet eye-catching.

Girls Can Lift Weights Too!

David Franks Sport Correspondent

Since 1896 at the Olympic Games in Athens, men have competed with each other in lifting weights. In 2000, at the Sydney Olympic Games, we saw women weightlifters for the first time.

Zoe Smith is one of many girls who dream of competing in the Olympic Games. However, not many choose weightlifting as their sport! Zoe is already Britain's strongest girl. She is 5ft 2in tall and weighs nine stone. She can already lift three times her own body weight.

She began lifting weights at the age of 12 and competed in the London Youth Games in 2006.

In 2008, she set 98 British records. She also won a gold medal in October at the Commonwealth Youth Games in Poona, in India. She could not compete in 2008 at the Beijing Olympics because athletes have to be 16 to enter the Olympic weightlifting competition.

She competes in two types of lifting. The first is called the 'snatch'. This is when the lifter uses one quick, uninterrupted movement to lift the weight. The other is the 'clean and jerk'. This is when the lifter brings the weight up so far, steadies and then 'jerks' the weight over the head. Zoe has lifted 59kg in the snatch and 90kg in the clean and jerk.

Brian Green, an expert on weightlifting, said, 'What Zoe has achieved is remarkable. We are very excited about her prospects in the next Olympic Games. China has always dominated women's weightlifting but I think Zoe could come away with a medal.'

Understanding the article

1 Who wrote the article?

2 What is it about?

3 Why did Zoe not take part in the 2008 Olympic Games?

4 What is the heaviest weight Zoe has lifted in:
   a the snatch   **b** the clean and jerk?

Looking at words

5 Explain the meaning of the words as they are used in the article:
   a uninterrupted   **b** steadies   **c** remarkable
   d prospects   **e** dominated

Exploring further

6 Why do you think men competed in weightlifting years before women did?

7 Why do you think weightlifters have to be 16 before they can compete at the Olympics?

8 Pick out an example of:
   a a fact   **b** an opinion.

9 How many paragraphs are there in the article?
What is each one about?

10 Why do you think Brian Green was quoted in the article?

Extra

Think about the three newspaper articles you have read.

• Choose the one you liked best.

• Write a paragraph to say why you found it interesting.

Quieter Than Snow

I went to school a day too soon
And couldn't understand
Why silence hung in the yard like sheets
Nothing to flap or spin, no creaks
Or shocks of voices, only air.

And the car park empty of teachers' cars
Only the first September leaves
Dropping like paper. No racks of bikes
No kicking legs, no fights,
No voices, laughter, anything.

Yet the door was open. My feet
Sucked down the corridor. My reflection
Walked with me past the hall.
My classroom smelt of nothing. And the silence
Rolled like thunder in my ears.

At every desk a child stared at me
Teachers walked through walls and back again
Cupboard doors swung open, and out crept
More silent children, and still more.

They tiptoed round me
Touched me with ice-cold hands
And opened up their mouths with laughter
That was

Quieter than snow.

Quieter than Snow, Berlie Doherty

- When did the poet go to school?
- What was the poet expecting to see and hear at school?
- What did the poet see outside?
- What did the poet see in the classroom?
- What does the poet say:
  • the silence was like
  • the leaves were like?
- The poet says: 'My feet sucked down the corridor.' What impression does the word 'sucked' give you?
- Who do you think the children and teachers are?
- How do you think the poet felt:
  • when she arrived at school
  • when she was in the classroom?
- How does the poem make you feel?
- If you could talk to these children, what would you say? What would you want to know?

The Hills

Sometimes I think the hills
That loom across the harbour
Lie there like sleeping dragons,
Crouched one above another,
With trees for tufts of fur
Growing all up and down
The ridges and humps of their backs,
And orange cliffs for claws
Dipped in the sea below.

 Understanding the poem
- What does the poet think the hills could be?
- What do the trees look like?
- What do the orange cliffs look like?
- What are they dreaming of?
- What does the poet wonder about in the last four lines of the poem?

Looking at words
Explain the meaning of these words as they are used in the poem:
a loom   **b** crouched   **c** wisp   **d** hollows   **e** stir   **f** clustered

Sometimes a wisp of smoke
Rises out of the hollows,
As if in their dragon sleep
They dreamed of strange old battles.
What if the hills should stir
Some day and stretch themselves,
Shake off the clinging trees
And all the clustered houses?

The Hills, Rachel Field

Understanding similes and metaphors

- The hills the poet is describing are 'across the harbour'. Do you think they are very near or at a distance?
- If the poet walked towards the hills, would they look:
  a more like dragons   **b** less like dragons?
  Explain your answer.
- What do you think the 'wisp of smoke' could be in the poet's imagination? What is it really?
- Why do you think the dragons would be dreaming of 'old battles'?
- How do you think the poet would feel if, one day, 'the hills should stir'?

Extra

Look out of your classroom window and half close your eyes. You may be looking at buildings or fields, trees or roads. In your imagination what animal can you see? Describe the parts of your animal.

19

One Moment in Summer

The house is dropping swallows
one by one from under the gutter

they swoop and fall
on our heads as we queue
for ice cream.

It is so hot
that the long line of cars clogging the road
hums like a line of electric fires.

They shine and shimmer, stink of oil and warm seats
the children gaze out from their misted windows.

Trapped under glass
hair plastered down with sweat
gasping for air like frogs under ice.

The cars crawl round the curve
of the road, stuck in between the shop
and the café.

My ice cream is butterscotch and almond
Lizzie's is chocolate, Harriet's vanilla.

They are so delicious and cold
we lick them slowly, letting the long, cool flavours
slide down our tongues.

Inside the cars, the red-faced people
begin to boil.

The swallows flit and dart
rapid specks of blue, black and white
the summer flies at us
like an arrow.

One moment in Summer, David Harmer

Understanding the poem

1 In the poem, what are:

    a the poet and her friends doing?

    b the cars doing?

    c the people in the cars doing?

2 How do the cars smell?

3 What three flavours of ice cream do they buy?

4 How do the friends eat the ice creams?

5 What colours are the swallows?

Looking at words

6 Explain the meaning of the words as they are used in the poem:

    a swoop   **b** clogging   **c** gasping

    d flit   **e** dart

Looking at words that create images

7 How does the poet describe:

    a the long line of cars   **b** the people in the cars?

8 Make a list of all the:

    a 'cold' words the poet uses   **b** 'hot' words the poet uses.

9 Why has the poet used so many 'hot' words in the poem?

10 Look at the title of the poem. Do you think it is a good title or not? Give your reasons.

Extra

Write a short description called 'One Moment in Winter'.
It is very cold. You and your friends are queuing for hot drinks.
The traffic is moving very slowly because there is lots of snow.
Use as many 'cold' words as you can in your description.

Let's find out about
Argentina

Location

Argentina is the second largest country in South America. It is long and thin with a 4,989 kilometre **coastline** which joins the Atlantic Ocean. It has borders with Bolivia, Brazil, Chile, Paraguay and Uruguay.

Terrain

Much of the northern part of the country is 'pampas'. This is an Indian word meaning a flat, **featureless** area. Along the western border of the country are the Andes. The highest point in this mountain range is Cerro Aconcagua which rises to 6,960 metres. There can be earthquakes in this part of the Andes.

Climate

Most of the country has a **temperate** climate. However, the south east is **arid** and the south west very cold, as this is the nearest point to the Antarctic. Violent wind storms can hit the northern part of the country.

The people

The **population** of Argentina is estimated to be 40 million. The official language is Spanish but Italian, English, German and French are also widely spoken. As Argentina **exports** wheat, maize and enormous quantities of meat, many people work on the land.

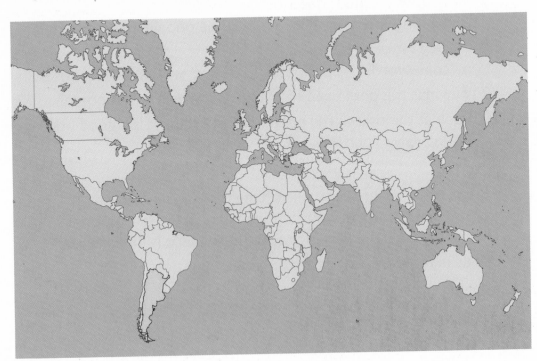

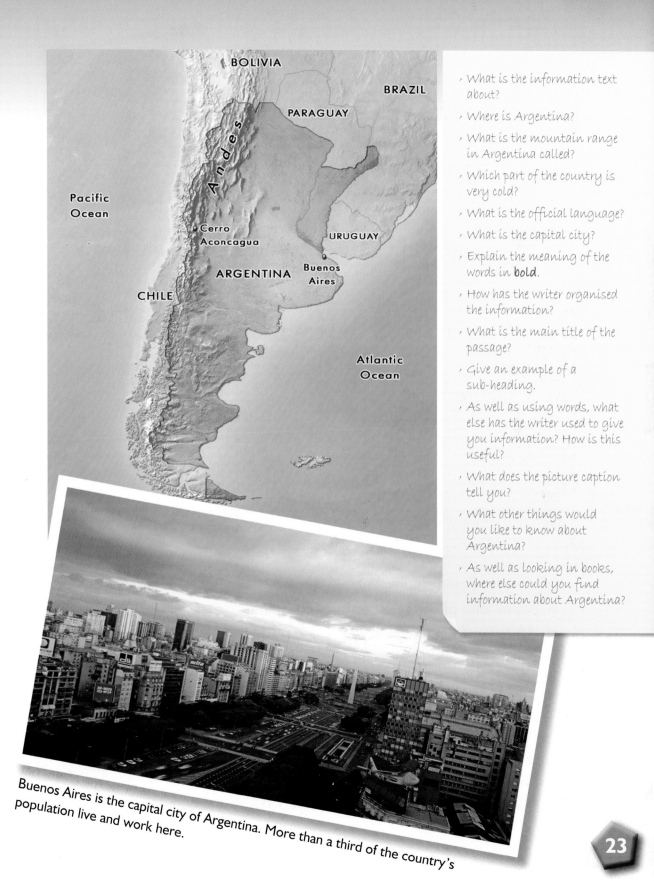

Buenos Aires is the capital city of Argentina. More than a third of the country's population live and work here.

- What is the information text about?
- Where is Argentina?
- What is the mountain range in Argentina called?
- Which part of the country is very cold?
- What is the official language?
- What is the capital city?
- Explain the meaning of the words in **bold**.
- How has the writer organised the information?
- What is the main title of the passage?
- Give an example of a sub-heading.
- As well as using words, what else has the writer used to give you information? How is this useful?
- What does the picture caption tell you?
- What other things would you like to know about Argentina?
- As well as looking in books, where else could you find information about Argentina?

Let's find out about
China

Location

China's official name is The People's Republic of China. It is in eastern Asia with coastlines along the East China Sea, the Yellow Sea, the Korea Bay and the South China Sea. It shares borders with many other countries including India and Russia.

Terrain

China is a very mountainous country with high plateaus. There are deserts in the west of the country and hills in the east. Mount Everest, the highest mountain in the world, is on China's border with Nepal.

Understanding the information

- What is China's official name?
- Name one of the seas along its coastline.
- Where are China's deserts?
- What is the climate like in the north of the country?
- What is China's main language?

Looking at words

Explain the meaning of these words as they are used in the text:

a official	**b** mountainous	**c** plateaus
d tropical	**e** frequent	**f** typhoons

Climate

China is a huge country and has many different climates. It is tropical in the south and very cold in the north. It has frequent typhoons along its southern and eastern coasts. It experiences droughts, floods and tsunamis.

The people

The population of China is over a billion people. Its main language is standard Chinese or Mandarin but many other dialects, such as Cantonese, are spoken. Its capital city is Beijing where the 2008 Olympic Games were held.

Exploring further

- Why do you think the writer has used sub-headings? Are they useful or not? Why?
- Why do you think the writer has shown two maps?
- What have you found out about Mount Everest?
- What other information could the writer have included that you would find interesting?

Extra

Choose a country that you are interested in or have visited.
Make a list of questions showing what information you would like to know about that country.

Let's find out about
Australia

Location

Australia is in the southern hemisphere. Its coastline is 25,760 kilometres in length and it does not border any other country.

Terrain

Australia is mostly low plateaus, and deserts cover most of the land away from the coast. It has a fertile plain in the south-east. Just off the coastline to the east can be found the Great Barrier Reef. This is the largest coral reef in the world.

Climate

Most of Australia has a very arid climate. Towards the south it is more temperate, with a climate similar to places like Spain and Italy. The north has a tropical climate. Sometimes there are serious cyclones along the coast, bringing floods and causing damage. The country often experiences drought.

The people

The population of Australia is just over 21 million. Europeans began to explore Australia in the 17th century. Many of the people today are descended from European settlers and about 79 per cent of the population speaks English. Other languages include Chinese, Italian and Greek.

The Great Barrier Reef

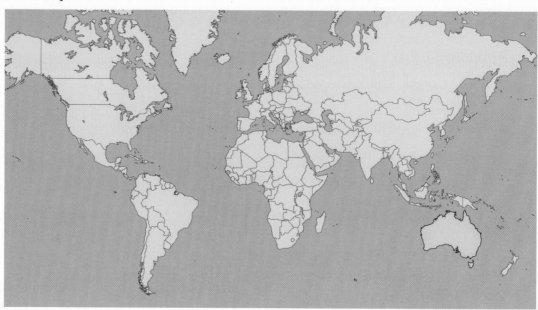

Understanding the information

1 Where is Australia?

2 Where is the Great Barrier Reef?

3 What sort of climate does most of Australia have?

4 How many people live there?

5 What language do most of the people speak?

Looking at words

6 Explain the meaning of the words and phrases in as they are used in the text:

    a hemisphere   **b** fertile   **c** coral reef
    d cyclones   **e** descended from

Exploring further

7 In what ways has the writer presented the information?

8 How do you know that Australia is an island?

9 Where do you think most of the food is grown?

10 Where do you think most of the people in Australia live?

Extra

These are three of the main cities in Australia:

- Canberra
- Sydney
- Melbourne

Choose one of these cities.

What information would you like to know about this city?

Make a list of questions. Can you find the answers?

27

Webbo

Davy has arrived at Webbo's school in Liverpool, and Webbo has decided he's an easy target for bullying.

Why me? Why had he taken such an instant dislike to me?

The term's first rounders match had got me off to a bad start, of course. I remember Webbo yelling 'Get it!' Well, how was I to know Lianne Whalley would sky the ball straight at me just when I was busy watching the seagulls pecking the leftover crisps off the Infants' yard? I didn't ask to be in the **vital** place at the last match-deciding moment. Five rounders each and only my hands between victory and defeat.

'Catch the thing!' bawled Webbo as he raced toward me. I didn't, of course. I tried. I stuck out my hands and did my best to cup them under the ball. I suppose my big chance to be a hero was just too much for me. I closed my eyes and hoped for the best, but the ball popped out of my hands as easily as it had dropped in. Lianne completed the rounder with her arms raised in **triumph**, while Pete Moran laughed himself sick at my attempt at a catch. Webbo wasn't laughing. He only played to win, and I'd just **scuppered** his hopes. Webbo didn't like being on the losing side – *ever*.

'You,' hissed Webbo, prodding a finger into my chest. 'You are dead.'

No, he definitely did not like being on the losing side. I looked around. Nobody was listening, nobody except Craig, and he just **grimaced** sympathetically.

'Try to keep out of Webbo's way,' he advised on the way back into school.

That was **easier said than done**. I'd realized on my first day since the move from Yorkshire a few months back that Webbo and I weren't going to get on.

'Hey, Woollyback,' he had shouted in the playground.

I must have looked blank.

'Yes, you,' he said. 'Don't you know what a Woollyback is?'

I shook my head. That was a mistake.

'Well, soft lad,' explained Webbo. 'It's like this. There are two kinds of people in the world, Scousers and Woollybacks. If you don't come from Liverpool, then you're a Woollyback. You're not from Liverpool, are you?'

No, I wasn't. I'd finally discovered that I had **something in common** with Michael Jackson, Arnold Schwarzenegger, the Pope and Mother Teresa of Calcutta – we're all Woollybacks!

'So now you understand, don't you, Woollyback?'

I nodded and turned to walk away. Carl O'Rourke barred my way.

'Who said you could go?' **demanded** Webbo.

'Nobody,' I admitted. Silly me, I didn't know I needed **permission**!

'Then you wait till you're told you can go,' said Webbo. 'Understand?'

'Yes,' I murmured nervously. 'I understand.'

Chicken, Alan Gibbons

- Who are the main characters?
- What are the two reasons why Webbo does not like the narrator?
- Why didn't Davy catch the ball? Why was Davy's catch so important?
- When did Davy realise that he and Webbo were not going to get on?
- Explain the meaning of the words and phrases in **bold**.
- How can you tell that Craig is not a member of Webbo's gang but Carl is?
- Do you think that Webbo has good reasons for disliking Davy? Why or why not?
- How do you think Davy feels about Webbo?
- How would you describe the sort of person Webbo is?

Trouble with Miss Gratwick

Miss Gratwick has taken a disliking to Mike Pilkington, and, one day, when she tells him off unfairly in front of the class, Mike becomes resentful and talks to his friend Chas about getting back at her.

'Pilkington,' said Miss Gratwick, 'is one of those mean and sneaky boys who call out behind their teacher's back.'

She had a very scathing voice, Miss Gratwick. Mike looked sulky. He didn't mind being ticked off if he deserved it, but this was unfair. He'd actually been trying to *help* Miss Gratwick. He'd been on her *side*. Chas had been prodding him in the back and trying to talk to him, and he had turned round to tell him to *shut up*, and this was the thanks he got.

Miss Gratwick turned as if to go on writing on the blackboard, but swung round again on the chance of catching him grinning at his friends. She was suspicious by nature.

But Mike hadn't moved. The class giggled, and Miss Gratwick felt foolish.

She snapped, 'And you can take that nasty look off your face!'

Gleefully, Chas poked him in the back.

'Sneaky boys, sneaky boys,' he whispered. 'Pilkington is one of those mean and sneaky boys …'

Mike edged away and ignored him.

Understanding the passage

- What does Miss Gratwick accuse Mike of doing?
- Why does Mike think it is unfair?
- Who should Miss Gratwick have been cross with?
- What does Mike do that really gets him into trouble?
- How does Miss Gratwick punish Mike?

Looking at words

Explain the meaning of these words and phrases as they are used in the story:

a scathing **b** ticked off **c** suspicious
d by nature **e** got it in for you **f** bitterness

'Neek-y boys, neek-y boys,' said Chas delightedly under his breath. 'Pil-king-ton is wunna-those-mean 'n' neek-y boys ...'

Mike turned suddenly and swiped at Chas's face.

'Oh, shut up!'

'Pilkington,' said Miss Gratwick, 'I've had just about enough of you. Come out!'

She gave Mike a painful knock on the head with the knuckle of her bony forefinger, and made him stand behind the blackboard for the rest of the lesson.

'She's got it in for you,' said Chas, as they left school.

'I've got it in for her and all.'

'What you reckon you're going to do, then?'

'You'll see.'

'What?'

'Not going to tell you.'

'I'll believe it when it happens.'

Mike's heart was full of bitterness. He would have liked to murder Miss Gratwick. But he choked back his feelings and changed the subject.

The Hallowe'en Cat, Kenneth Lillington

Exploring further

- What sort of person do you think Miss Gratwick is?
- How do you think she treats Mike?
- What sort of person do you think Chas is?
- How do you know that Mike and Chas are friends? Do you think this is odd?
- Why do you think Mike will not tell Chas what he is going to do?

Extra

If you were in Mike's position, what would you do? What would be a sensible way to try to get Miss Gratwick to stop picking on you? Why might this be a difficult thing to do?

The Balaclava Boys

The narrator of this story wants a balaclava so he can be part of the 'Balaclava Boys'. There is only one problem – his mum won't let him have one!

I knew exactly the kind of balaclava I wanted. One just like Tony's, a sort of yellowy-brown. His dad had given it to him because of his earache. Mind you, he didn't like wearing it at first. At school he'd given it to Barry to wear and got it back before home-time. But all the other lads started asking if they could have a wear of it, so Tony took it back and said that from then on nobody but him could wear it, not even Barry. Barry told him he wasn't bothered because he was going to get a balaclava of his own, and so did some of the other lads. And that's how it started – the Balaclava Boys.

It wasn't a gang really. I mean they didn't have meetings or anything like that. They just went around together wearing their balaclavas, and if you didn't have one you couldn't go around with them. Tony and Barry were my best friends, but because I didn't have a balaclava, they wouldn't let me go round with them. I tried.

'Aw, go on, Barry, let us walk round with you.'

'No, you can't. You're not a Balaclava Boy.'

'Aw, go on.'

'No.'

'Please.'

I don't know why I wanted to walk round with them anyway. All they did was wander up and down the playground dressed in their rotten balaclavas. It was daft.

'Go on, Barry, be a sport.'

'I've told you. You're not a Balaclava Boy. You've got to have a balaclava. If you get one, you can join.'

'But I can't, Barry. My mum won't let me have one.'

'Hard luck.'

'You're rotten.'

Then he went off with the others. I wasn't half fed up. All my friends were in the Balaclava Boys. All the lads in my class except me. Wasn't fair. The bell went for the next lesson – ooh heck, handicraft with the Miseryguts Garnett – then it was home-time. All the Balaclava Boys were going in and I followed them.

'Hey, Tony, do you want to go down to the woods after school?'
'No, I'm going round with the Balaclava Boys.'
'Oh.'
Blooming Balaclava Boys. Why wouldn't *my mum* buy *me a balaclava?* Didn't she realize that I was losing all my friends, and just because she wouldn't buy me one?

The Balaclava Story, George Layton

Understanding the passage

1 Why did Tony's dad give Tony a balaclava?
2 Who were the narrator's best friends?
3 What did the 'Balaclava Boys' do together?
4 Why didn't the narrator have a balaclava?
5 What didn't his mother realise?

Looking at words

6 Explain the meaning of these words and phrases as they are used in the story:

   a bothered   b rotten   c daft
   d be a sport   e fed up   f handicraft

Exploring further

7 Tony didn't like his balaclava at first. What made him change his mind?

8 The narrator says that what the Balaclava Boys did was 'daft'. How do you know he didn't really mean this?

9 Why do you think it was so important to the narrator that he had a balaclava?

10 The boys in balaclavas went around together. Do you think this is a sensible way to choose your friends? Why? Why not?

Extra

Imagine you are the narrator. You have to explain to your mum why you want a balaclava and persuade her to buy you one.
Write what you would say.

How Does Your Heart Work?

What is the heart?

The heart is a **crucial** organ of the body. It pumps blood through the small tubes that we call veins and arteries. Without blood we could not **survive**.

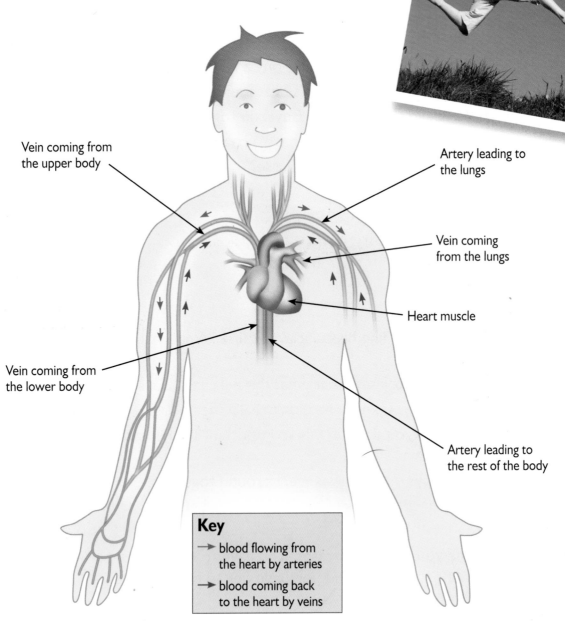

Vein coming from the upper body

Artery leading to the lungs

Vein coming from the lungs

Heart muscle

Vein coming from the lower body

Artery leading to the rest of the body

Key

→ blood flowing from the heart by arteries

→ blood coming back to the heart by veins

34

How does it work?

- One artery takes blood from the heart to the lungs.

- When the blood reaches the lungs it picks up oxygen. It leaves carbon dioxide behind in the lungs.

- The blood with the oxygen goes back to the heart.

- The other artery takes the blood with the oxygen all around the body.

- After the oxygen has been **delivered**, veins bring the blood back to the heart.

- The **process** starts all over again.

- One artery takes blood from the heart to the lungs …

And so the heart pumps the blood around our body, supplying the oxygen that is **essential** to keep us fit and healthy.

> - What does the heart do to the blood?
> - What does the blood travel through?
> - Where do arteries take the blood?
> - Where do veins take the blood?
> - What does the blood take from the lungs? What does it leave?
> - Explain the meaning of the words in **bold**.
> - What is the purpose of this piece of writing?
> - How is the information presented?
> - Why do you think the writer has used:
>   - sub-headings
>   - bullet points?
> - Is the diagram useful? Why? Why not?
> - Did you find this easy to understand or not? Explain your reasons.

How Do We Move?

This is what it looks like inside your arm.

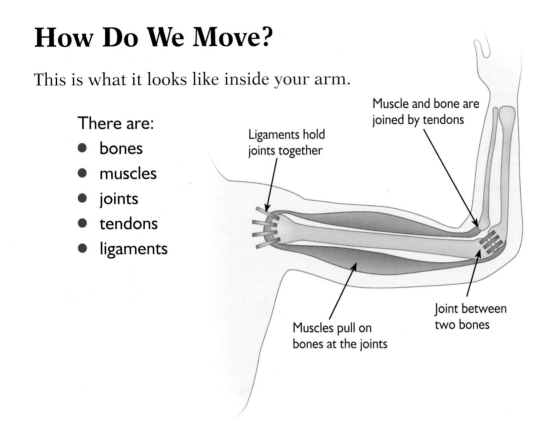

There are:
- bones
- muscles
- joints
- tendons
- ligaments

Ligaments hold joints together

Muscle and bone are joined by tendons

Muscles pull on bones at the joints

Joint between two bones

 Understanding the explanation
- Name the parts inside your arm.
- What is it called where two bones meet?
- What do ligaments do?
- Do muscles work alone?
- When the parts inside your arm work together, what can you do?

Looking at words

Use a dictionary to find the definitions for these words:

a tendons   **b** ligaments   **c** contracts   **d** relaxes

Here is how all these parts work together so you can move your arm. Muscles work in pairs. Muscles A and B work together. Muscles C and D work together.

- **When we want to move our arm downwards, one muscle contracts and the other muscle relaxes.** Look at muscles A and B.

muscle A relaxes

muscle C contracts

muscle B contracts

muscle D relaxes

- **When we want to move our arm upwards, one muscle contracts and the other muscle relaxes.** Look at muscles C and D.

Exploring further

- What is the purpose of this piece of writing?
- Who do you think would want to read this?
- How is the information presented?
- Would the explanation be as easy to understand without the diagrams? Why? Why not?

Extra

Your leg works in the same way as your arm.

- Move the bottom half of your leg upwards. Which muscle is contracting and which muscle is relaxing?
- Move the bottom part of your leg downwards. Which muscle is contracting and which muscle is relaxing?
- Draw a diagram to explain what you have found out.

How Do Our Lungs Work?

This is what it looks like
inside your chest.

There are:
● lungs
● windpipe
● heart
● ribs
● muscles

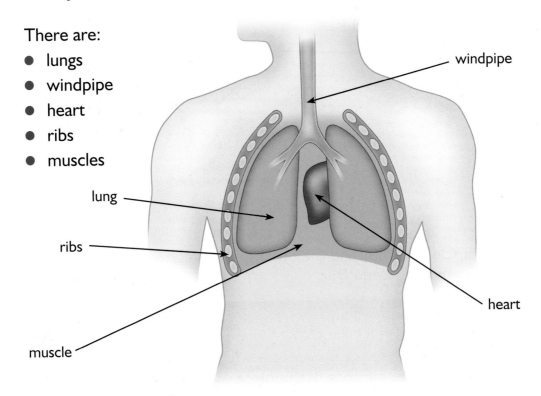

windpipe

lung

ribs

heart

muscle

The lungs are the organs in the body that allow us to breathe. They are
like balloons. They can expand and contract.

This is how it works.
● We breathe in and our lungs fill with air and expand.
● Blood comes from the heart and:
  – picks up the oxygen from the air in our lungs
  – delivers carbon dioxide to the lungs.
● We breathe out and our lungs contract.
● When we breathe out, we get rid of the carbon dioxide.

The grass was dry and scratchy, but they were used to it. Now and again, a car or a truck roared by, and then the road was quiet again and they were alone. Naledi began to sing the words of her favourite tune and Tiro was soon joining in.

On they walked.

'Can't we stop and eat?' Tiro was beginning to feel sharp stabs of hunger. But Naledi wanted to go on until they reached the top of the long, low hill ahead.

Their legs slowed as they began the walk uphill, their bodies feeling heavy. At last they came to the top and flopped down to rest.

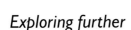

Hungrily they ate their sweet potatoes and drank the water. The air was hot and still. Some birds skimmed lightly across the sky as they gazed down at the long road ahead. It stretched into the distance, between fenced-off fields and dry grass, up to another far-off hill.

'Come on! We must get on,' Naledi insisted, pulling herself up quickly.

She could tell that Tiro was already tired, but they couldn't afford to stop for long. The sun had already passed its midday position and they didn't seem to have travelled very far.

On they walked, steadily, singing to break the silence.

Journey to Jo'burg, Beverley Naidoo

Exploring further
- Which of the children do you think is older? Why?
- Why do you think they sang as they walked?
- How do you know that they had been walking for more than an hour?
- Why do you think the author repeats 'On they walked'?
- Do you think they will make it to Johannesburg? Why? Why not?

At the time of this story, Naledi and Tiro faced very special dangers. You can read about their courage and whether they find their mother and save their little sister in *Journey to Jo'burg* by Beverley Naidoo.

Extra

Imagine you are going on a long journey on foot. Think about:
a how you plan the journey   **b** what you would take with you.
Remember! You have to carry anything you take with you.

My Home

Juan describes the beautiful scenery, animals, the people and life in the place where he was born – his home town, San Pablo.

My name is Juan. I live in Guatemala, in the mountains. My town, San Pablo, has three huge volcanoes near it, and high cliffs all around it, and steep, bright green fields of corn and garlic and onions growing in the hills, and red coffee berries growing in the shade of big trees in the valleys. It has lots of flowers and birds – eagles and orioles and owls, hummingbirds, and flocks of wild parrots that zoom down out of the trees to steal our corn and don't talk any language but their own.

San Pablo is on a big lake with seven other towns around it. People get from one town to another mostly by ferry-boat or canoe. There's a road, but it's not a good one.

I've never been in any of the other towns, only San Pablo. Still, at night I like to go down to the lake and look at the lights of the fishing canoes on the black water, and the lights of the other towns glowing at us across the lake, and the thousands of stars in the sky. It seems like every light is saying, 'You're not alone. We're here too.'

Right in town, San Pablo has stray dogs and dust in the street, and a few cars, and a few buses from the big cities, and a few mules carrying firewood from the mountains, and lots of people carrying still more stuff – jugs of water or big baskets of bread or vegetables on their heads, babies on their backs, or sometimes huge wooden beams balanced over their shoulders – whatever they need to take home. Since there aren't many cars, if you want something, you carry it yourself, no matter how heavy it is.

The only time people aren't carrying things is at night, when they go out just to stroll around town and have fun and tell stories and talk to their friends. Everybody walks in the street, more or less straight down the middle, and if a car comes while

somebody's having a good conversation or telling a good story, the car has to wait till the story finishes before the people will move out of the way. Stories are important here, and cars aren't.

Down by the beach there's an especially beautiful place – a big, low house with lots of windows, and flowers and palm trees all around, and green grass and peacocks in the yard, and an iron gate that opens for walking right down to the water.

That's where I was born.

The Most Beautiful Place in the World, Ann Cameron

Understanding the passage

1 Give two examples from the passage of:
   a things that grow in the hills
   b birds
   c things that people carry.
2 How do people get from town to town?
3 Why don't they use the road?
4 What do people do at night in San Pablo?
5 Why does Juan say that the house on the beach is an 'especially beautiful place'?

Looking at words

6 Explain the meaning of these words as they are used in the passage:
   a zoom   **b** stray dogs   **c** mules
   d beams   **e** stroll

Exploring settings

7 Could San Pablo be a dangerous place to live? Why?
8 Do you think Juan would like to visit other towns or not? Explain your reasons.
9 How can you tell San Pablo has a hot climate?
10 Do you think San Pablo is a rich town or a poor town? Give your reasons.

Extra

Explain what you like about San Pablo and what you don't like about it.

WINNER – Best Motion Picture ★ WINNER – Best Actor ★ WINNER – Best **Soundtrack**

'SUPERB! If you only see one film this year, see **BIGFOOT**'. (*The Daily News*)

'Gripping – it will keep you on the edge of your seat!' (*The World*)

Starring   SEBASTIAN CONWAY   ELLA PRINCE   BRAD EVANS

BIGFOOT

In the frozen wastes of North America, a man comes face to face with a legend.
He has hunted and found Bigfoot. But now, the tables are turned and
the hunter becomes the hunted!

BASED ON THE BOOK BY **JOHN REEVE**

12A

BIGFOOT

A large ape-like creature has been
spotted in North America.
Is this just another hoax
or does Bigfoot really exist?

Explorer and adventurer Sam Grant
is determined to find out.
He will hunt Bigfoot
and bring it back alive!

But his adventure turns into a deadly battle
with the monster! Who will win?
Who will survive?

Praise for John Reeve's *Bigfoot*
'The best book I've read this year'.
'A real page turner'.
'I read it in one go – I couldn't put it down'.

0 123456 789

- What is the title of the film and the book?
- Who is the author of the book?
- Who is starring in the film?
- Who can go to see the film?
- Who is the main character in the book?
- Explain the meaning of the words and phrases: Soundtrack, gripping, legend, tables are turned, hoax, deadly, page-turner.
- Why does the film advert include awards and quotes from newspapers?
- What sort of people do you think would go to see this film?
- Would the advert persuade you to see the film or not?
- Why does the book blurb ask questions but give no answers?
- Why do you think the book blurb does not tell you the end of the story?
- Look at 'Praise for John Reeve's Bigfoot.' Do these comments make you want to read the book? Why? Why not?
- What are the film advert and the book blurb trying to do?

Unit
8

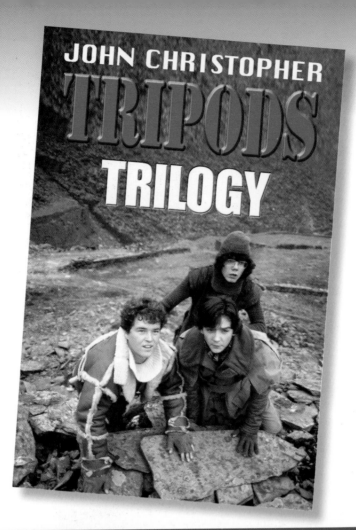

Understanding the book cover and blurb

- What is the book called?
- Who is the author?
- Where could you watch a series based on the book?
- What is the name of the machines that rule the Earth?
- Who is the main character in the book?

Looking at words

Explain the meaning of these words and phrases as they are used in the book blurb:

a alien　　**b** enslaved　　**c** ritual　　**d** rebel

e overthrow　　**f** very slim　　**g** unbearably

The Tripods are Coming!

The Tripods are Coming!

THE TRIPODS ARE HERE!

Massive, alien machines, the Tripods had ruled Earth for hundreds of years and enslaved the minds and bodies of most adults through the silvery caps they made them wear.

Determined to escape the ritual Capping ceremony, Will Parker runs away, heading for the distant White Mountains and the small rebel camp there, hoping to join their desperate attempts to overthrow the rule of the Tripods. The journey is long, the missions dangerous and the hope of surviving very slim …

John Christopher's almost unbearably exciting trilogy appears for the first time in one volume:

**The White Mountains,
The City of Gold and Lead,
The Pool of Fire**

0 123456 789010

Exploring further

- Does the cover illustration make you interested in the book? Why? Why not?
- Look at the yellow, orange and red lines of the book blurb. Do they make you want to read on or not? Explain your reasons.
- What will the 'ritual Capping ceremony' do to Will?
- Why do you think the author tells you that the rebels' hope of surviving is 'very slim'?
- Why do you think the writer has used these words:
  'thrilling', 'dangerous', 'unbearably exciting'?
- Does the book cover and blurb want to make you read the book? Why? Why not?

Extra

Using the information on the book cover and in the blurb, make a newspaper advert for the TV series.

A magical film that the whole family will enjoy. The scenery is beautiful and the monster so realistic you feel you could reach out and touch it!

Search for the LOCH NESS MONSTER

Starring the award-winning **Anne Grey** and **John Johnson**

Maggie Brown's holiday on the banks of Loch Ness is more than she bargained for!

She sees the legendary Loch Ness Monster but no one believes her.

Can she convince people that she is not going mad?

12A

'A superb performance from Anne Grey.' (The World)
'One of the best films I've seen in years.' (Film Review)

Understanding the advert

   1 Who are the stars of the film?

   2 Where is the film set?

   3 Who is the main character?

   4 Who can go to see the film?

Looking at words

   5 Explain the meaning of these words and phrases as they are used in the advert:

   a magical   **b** award-winning

   c more than she bargained for   **d** legendary

   e convince   **f** performance

Exploring persuasive texts

   6 Find the question in the advert. Why do you think it asks that question?

   7 Why do you think the advert includes quotes from newspapers?

   8 Why do you think it does not include quotes from people who did not like the film?

   9 Why do you think it is important that the monster is 'realistic'?

   10 Would the advert persuade you to see the film? Why? Why not?

Extra

Imagine that *Search for the Loch Ness Monster* is a book. Write a book blurb to persuade people to read the book.

The Lake

Children from dying Earth have arrived in a spacecraft to settle on a new planet which they name Shine …

Before us lay a wide and gentle **plain** sloping to the shores of a round wide lake some miles across. Beyond the lake, a very high mountain with perfectly **symmetrical** slopes rose into the sky, topped with snow. A mirror image of the lovely mountain hung **inverted** in the lake, quite still, for the surface was like glass, perfectly **unruffled** by even the slightest impulse of the air. The surface of the plain was grey and silver, shining like **marcasite** in places, in others with a pewter sheen. To the left and the right of the plain, on gentle hills, were wide sweeps of woodland, with quite recognizable and normal trees, except that the leaves upon them were not green but shades of red, and shining, like the blaze of an amazing autumn. It was very beautiful, and perfectly silent, and perfectly still.

The children ran forward onto the open expanse of land before them, shouting. And at once we were limping, crying, and hopping back. We were still wearing the soft ship slippers we had been given to keep down the noise in the corridors of the spacecraft, and the pretty grey grass and flowers had cut through the thin leather at once, and cut our feet. The Guide ordered the crate of boots to be brought from the store and unpacked. Someone fetched ointment and sticking plaster. Meanwhile, we stooped and picked the sharp plants, which broke easily in our fingers when gathered; they seemed to be made of glass, sharp and shining like jewels. But as soon as we all had boots on, we could walk over them safely, for the growth was crushed beneath the soles, as **fragile** and crunchy to walk on as the frost-stiffened grass of winter on Earth.

We all walked over the crisp and sparkling frost plain, down towards the shores of the lake. It took an hour to reach it. The lake shore was a wide silver beach, made of soft bright sand, like grains of worndown glass. And all the time we walked toward the lake, it did not move, or ruffle, even enough to shake the curtains of reflected mountain and reflected sky that hung in it. And though the air smelled good and sweet to breathe, it was windless, and as still as the air in a deep cave underground. Only the little rivulet that followed us across to the lake from the crag valley where the ship had lodged moved; it chuckled gently from stone to stone, and sparkled as brightly as the glass leaves and grass. When we got to the beach, Pattie went to look where it joined the lake, to see if it would make some splash or ripples for just a little way, but it seemed to slide beneath the surface at once and made only the faintest ripple ring, quickly dying in the brilliant mirror of the lake.

'I think we may be lucky,' said the Guide. 'I think this place is good.'

Shine, Jill Paton Walsh

› The spacecraft has landed on a new planet. What do the children do first?

› Why was that a dangerous thing to do?

› How did they solve the problem?

› What happened to the plants when the children picked them up?

› Find adjectives in the story that describe: the lake; the mountain; the plain; the hills.

› Explain the meaning of the words and phrases in **bold**.

› What things look like things on Earth? What things are different?

› What do you think is the most unusual thing about the planet?

› Why do you think the author uses lots of descriptions?

› Do you agree with the Guide that 'this place is good'? Explain your reasons.

Down the Rabbit Hole

Alice has been sitting by the river reading her book. Suddenly she sees something very strange – a White Rabbit runs by saying, 'Oh dear! Oh dear! I shall be too late.' Alice jumps up and follows the White Rabbit and finds herself falling down a rabbit hole! Down, down, down until she lands on a heap of sticks and dry leaves.

Alice was not a bit hurt, and she jumped up on to her feet in a moment; she looked up, but it was all dark overhead. Before her was another long passage and the White Rabbit was still in sight, hurrying down it. There was not a moment to be lost. Away went Alice like the wind, and she was just in time to see the Rabbit turn a corner and say, 'Oh my ears and whiskers, how late it's getting!' Alice was close behind it when she turned the corner, but the Rabbit was no longer to be seen.

She found herself in a long, low hall which was lit up by a row of lamps hanging from the roof. There were doors all around the hall, but they were all locked. When Alice had been all the way down one side and up the other, trying every door, she walked sadly down the middle, wondering how she was ever going to get out again.

Suddenly, she came upon a little three-legged table, all made of solid glass. There was

Understanding the passage

- What was the first unusual thing that happened?
- What did Alice do?
- Where did she find herself?
- What was on the table?
- Which door could Alice open?
- What was the difference between the hall and the garden?

Looking at phrases

Explain what the phrases mean as they are used in the passage:

a not a moment to be lost   **b** like the wind

c at any rate   **d** out-of-the-way things

(turning round) It's only just back there – at least – I'm not sure. It is summer there.

Faun: Meanwhile, it is winter in Narnia, and has been for ever so long, and we shall both catch cold if we stand here talking in the snow. Daughter of Eve from the far land of Spare Oom, where **eternal** summer **reigns** around the bright city of War Drobe, how would it be if you came and had tea with me?

Lucy: *(Lucy shakes her head)* Thank you very much, Mr Tumnus, but I was wondering whether I ought to be getting back.

Adapted from *The Lion, the Witch and the Wardrobe*, C S Lewis

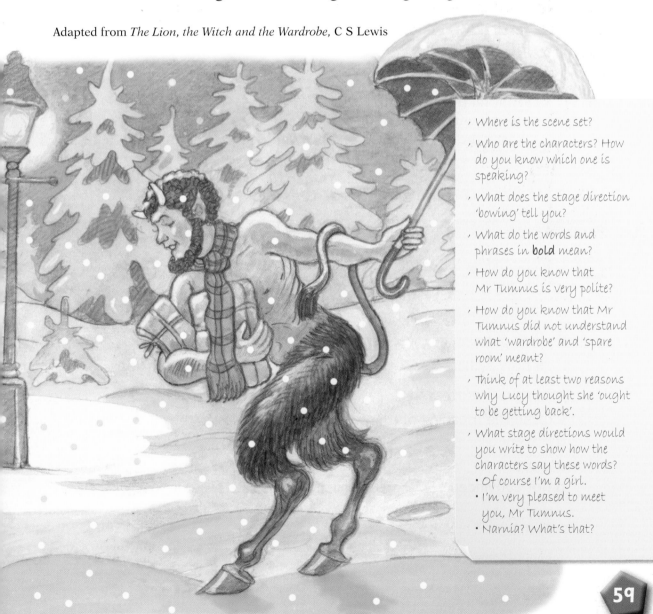

› Where is the scene set?
› Who are the characters? How do you know which one is speaking?
› What does the stage direction 'bowing' tell you?
› What do the words and phrases in **bold** mean?
› How do you know that Mr Tumnus is very polite?
› How do you know that Mr Tumnus did not understand what 'wardrobe' and 'spare room' meant?
› Think of at least two reasons why Lucy thought she 'ought to be getting back'.
› What stage directions would you write to show how the characters say these words?
  • Of course I'm a girl.
  • I'm very pleased to meet you, Mr Tumnus.
  • Narnia? What's that?

The threat

Davy is being bullied by Webbo and his mates. Mr Clarke, the teacher, senses that something is wrong.

Scene: A classroom. The lesson has just ended and the class are leaving.

Mr Clarke:	Davy? Pop over here a sec.
	Mr Clarke looks at Davy. Davy remains silent.
	Any problems, Davy?
Davy:	What do you mean Mr Clarke?
Mr Clarke:	Is somebody giving you a hard time?
	Davy shrugs.
	You don't seem very happy. You're not taking much care with your work, either. I've noticed a change over the last couple of weeks. Would you like to tell me about it?
	Davy sees Webbo peering through the classroom window. He lowers his eyes.

Understanding the scene
- Where is the scene set?
- Who are the characters?
- Pick out a stage direction that tells you:

    a how a character says something **b** what a character does.

Looking at words
Explain the meaning of these words and phrases as they are used in the scene:

a a sec	**b** a hard time	**c** shrugs
d not convinced	**e** menacingly	**f** get it

Mr Clarke:	Davy?
Davy:	Yes, Mr Clarke?
Mr Clarke:	I asked if you'd like to tell me about it? I want to help. *Davy remains silent.* I can't do anything unless you tell me what's wrong, you know. *Webbo and his mates are jabbing their fingers at Davy behind Mr Clarke's back.*
Davy:	*(mumbling)* There's nothing wrong.
Mr Clarke:	*(not convinced)* Sure? *(Davy nods.)* OK, off you go. *Outside the classroom. Webbo and his mates are waiting.*
Webbo:	What did Clarkey want?
Davy:	He asked me if anything was wrong.
Webbo:	What did you say?
Davy:	I said no.
Vincent:	You took a long time to say no.
Davy:	He kept asking me. I didn't say anything, honest.
Webbo:	*(menacingly)* Well, keep your mouth shut or you'll really get it.

Adapted from *Chicken* by Alan Gibbons

Exploring further

● What impression do you get of Mr Clarke?

● Why do you think Davy doesn't tell Mr Clarke what is wrong?

● Why do you think Webbo and his mates are 'jabbing their fingers' at Davy through the classroom window?

● If you had to write stage directions to show how the characters say these words, what would they be?

  a Any problems, Davy?   **b** What did Clarkey want?

  c I didn't say anything, honest.

Extra

Imagine that Davy goes back to Mr Clarke and tells him what is wrong. Mr Clarke tells Davy what he is going to do about it. Create, practise and perform the scene.

Staying together

During the Second World War, many cities were bombed so children were sent away to the country for safety. Carrie and Nick and other children have been sent to Wales.

Scene: A village hall, somewhere in Wales during the Second World War.
The children have been told to stand by the wall and wait for someone to choose them.

Carrie: *(bewildered)* What's happening?
Albert: *(sounding disgusted)* A kind of cattle auction, it seems.
                Albert sits on his suitcase and begins to read a book.
Woman: Nice little girl for Mrs Davies, now?
                Carrie and Nick hold hands tightly. They do not want to be separated.
Carrie: *(to Nick)* Why don't you smile and look nice!
                Nick blinks in surprise.
                Oh, it's all right, I'm not cross. I won't leave you.
                A few minutes pass and children are chosen and led away.
Woman: *(stopping in front of Carrie and Nick)*
                Surely you can take two, Mrs Evans?
Mrs Evans: Two girls, perhaps. Not a boy and a girl, I'm afraid. I've only one room, see, and my brother's particular.
Carrie: *(shyly)* Nick sleeps in my room at home because he has bad dreams sometimes. I always look after him and he's no trouble at all.
Mrs Evans: *(looking doubtful)* Well, I don't know what my brother will say. Perhaps I can chance it.
                She smiles at Carrie.
                There's pretty eyes you have, girl! Like green glass!
Carrie: *(smiling back)* Oh, Nick's the pretty one really.

Adapted from *Carrie's War* by Nina Bawden

Understanding the scene

1 When is the scene set?

2 Where is it set?

3 Who are the characters?

4 Pick out a stage direction that tells you:

    a how a character says something

    b what a character does.

Looking at words

5 Explain the meaning of these words as they are used in the scene:

    a bewildered   **b** auction   **c** separated

    d doubtful

Exploring further

6 How do you know that Albert is not impressed with what is happening?

7 Why do you think Carrie wants Nick to 'smile and look nice'?

8 What impression do you get of:

    a Mrs Evans   **b** Mrs Evans's brother?

9 How do you know that Nick is usually the one people take notice of?

10 If you had been one of the children waiting to be chosen, explain how you think you would have been feeling.

Extra

Imagine you are Carrie. Write a letter to your mother describing what happened in the village hall and how you felt about it.

How to use this book

This Pupil Book consists of ten units that help to teach comprehension skills for a range of different text types and genres, including fiction, non-fiction and poetry. It can be used on its own or as part of the whole Nelson Comprehension series, including Teacher's Resource Books and CD-ROMs. Each Nelson Comprehension unit is split into three sections.

Teach

The 'Teach' section includes an illustrated text for a teacher and children to read together and discuss in class. To help guide the discussion, a series of panel prompt questions is supplied, which can be used to help model a full range of comprehension skills (such as literal understanding, inference and evaluation). Full answer guidance is supplied in the accompanying *Teacher's Resource Book*, with multi-modal whiteboard support (complete with voiceovers and a range of audio and visual features) on the CD-ROM.

Talk

The aim of this section is to get the children in small groups to practise the skills they have just learnt. Each child could take on a role within the group, such as scribe, reader or advocate. They are presented with a range of questions to practise the skills they have been learning in the 'Teach' section.

The questions are followed up by a discussion, drama, role play or other group activity to further reinforce their learning. Further guidance is supplied in the *Teacher's Resource Book*, while interactive group activities to support some of the 'Talk' questions and activities are supplied on the CD-ROM.

Write

The third section offers an opportunity to test what the children have learnt by providing a new text extract and a series of questions, which can be answered orally, as a class exercise, or as an individual written exercise. The questions are colour coded according to their type, with initial literal questions, followed by vocabulary clarification, inference and evaluation questions and then an extended follow-up activity. Full answer guidance is supplied in the accompanying *Teacher's Resource Book*, while a whiteboard questioning reviewing feature is supplied on the CD-ROM.